Copyright © 2022 Matthew Douglas Pinard

All Rights Reserved. No part of this book publication may be reproduced or transmitted in any form or by any means, mechanical or electronic, including photocopying, scanning, and recording, or by any information storage and retrieval system, or other -- without prior permission in writing from the author or publisher. Disclaimers: The Publisher and the Author make no representation or warranties concerning the accuracy or completeness of the contents of this work and specifically disclaim all warranties for a particular purpose. No warranty may be created or extended through sales or promotional materials. The advice and strategies contained herein may not be suitable for every situation. This work is sold with the understanding that the Author and Publisher are not engaged in rendering legal, technological, or other professional services. If professional assistance is required, the services of a competent professional should be sought. Neither the Publisher nor the Author shall be liable for damages arising therefrom. The fact that an organization or website is referred to in this work as a citation and/or potential source of further information does not mean that the Author or the Publisher endorses the information, the organization, or website it may provide, or recommendations it may make. Further, readers should be aware that the websites listed in this work may have changed or disappeared between the time that this work was written and when it is read. Details of the cases and stories in this book have been changed to preserve privacy.

Printed in the United States of America
Published by: Writer's Publishing House
Prescott, Az 86301

Cover and Interior Design by Creative Artistic Excellence Marketing
Project Management and Book Launch by Creative Artistic Excellence Marketing
https://lizzymcnett.com

Paperback ISBN: 978-1-64873-261-4
Hardcover ISBN: 978-1-64873-262-1
Ebook ISBN: 978-1-64873-263-8

TABLE OF CONTENTS

THE SACRIFICIAL DEER	4
MOLLIE TIBBETTS	15
DOE MOUNTAIN	25
David Crawford	28
ANUNNAKI ANGELS HALF-HUMAN	35
"Beautiful Swan" and "Endless Life"	38
JAYME CLOSS	52
ARCHANGEL GABRIEL'S FOLDED WINGS	57
"BE LOVE" AND "BELIEVE"	73
PEACE TOWN	80
MISSING	91
MESSAGES FROM MOTHER ST. MARY	109
Boynton Canyon	120
TAXI ARCH	162
Taxi Arch	164
Other Books by Author Matthew	168
Screenplay Awards	171
Matthew Douglas Pinard	171

The Veil Rent

THE SACRIFICIAL DEER

In thinking how I wanted to start the third volume of The New Wine, I want to relay an incident that happened to my wife and I while driving from a "paranormal fest" in Petoskey, Michigan, on October 13, 2018. The very interesting thing about this accident was that it happened at exactly 7:00 p.m. in the evening. The number seven is a very spiritually significant and mystical number.

As we were driving home from this paranormal festival after meeting other mystics, psychics, and "spirit communers," our 2017 Chevy Equinox struck a large multipoint deer that seemed to appear out of nowhere. I have hit deer with cars before, even head on, and I have always seen the animal running from my peripheral vision. This deer appeared literally out of nowhere, and after it was struck, the paramedics and police could find absolutely no trace of it. The deer strike destroyed the entire engine block of our small SUV and thankfully did not permanently injure either my wife or I. What was interesting about the incident was that we had been debating all weekend about whether we should move out west from Michigan to Arizona, a place in which we love to vacation and always feel spiritually uplifted.

As we sat at a local gas station watching our totaled SUV be hauled away by a tow truck, we realized we had no way to make it back home two hours south to our house in Spring Lake, Michigan. We ended up calling our favorite restaurant, Hermann's German Café, in Cadillac, Michigan, and asked if there were any servers who wouldn't mind giving us a lift back home in exchange for some cash. We immediately were connected with an angelic woman named Kathy who volunteered to help us in our time of need.

As we were driving home in her car, Kathy turned to my wife Carol and said, "You are going to be moving out west very soon." I truly believe that Kathy, like myself and Carol, was also a mystic and prophet who did clearly see our future. As of the writing of this third volume of The New Wine, we are now pleased to say our new home is in central Arizona. As Jim Morrison and I used to sing, "The west is the best…get here and we'll do the rest."

Photo: An amazing sunset was given to us by St. Mary on December 15, 2018, as we left our home in West Michigan on our way to Prescott Valley, Arizona. This incredible sunset was further confirmation from on high that our move was fully supported by our Blessed Mother Mary.

Shortly before our permanent move west from Michigan to Arizona, I had two very powerful mystical, spiritual experiences I will document with photographs below.

The first experience was while praying for Carol's aunt Jo Ann Powers, who was an amazing blues singer and also Detroit native and former resident of Arizona. Jo Ann had passed away a few years ago from terminal brain cancer. My wife Carol asked if I could ask St. Mary to find out if Jo Ann was in heaven and no longer suffering.

After a full rosary at St. Patrick's Catholic Church in Grand Haven, Michigan, I was shown an image of Jo Ann Powers singing loudly at what appeared to me in my mind as a "feast of all saints." A few days after receiving this image, my wife took an incredible photograph of a woman's face in the sunset that also appeared to be a woman with a lion's face.

Photo: This incredible "lion face sunset" photo appeared a few days after my wife Carol asked me to ask St. Mary to show us where her aunt Jo Ann Powers was currently at following her death from brain cancer. Jo Ann was an extraordinary blues singer based out of Phoenix, Arizona. After praying at a local Catholic church, this image appeared a few days later, and my wife snapped the photo in the skies of West Michigan. It appears as a female lion with long eyelashes. (JoAnn had lovely long eyelashes.)

    The other amazing experience I had was an intuition that as I was anxiously waiting for The New Wine Volume 2 to be published which directly revealed the identity of the fallen entity who had been harassing many of us, I told my local parish priest Fr. Dave Gross of St. Mary's Catholic Church of Spring Lake, Michigan, I believed we would be getting a sign in the skies. The prayer I had been reciting was for Lucifer/ Hillel Ben Shachar/Memnoch/Satan/red dragon, devil, and all his evil "lions of the night" to not be able to harass, possess, control, influence, or affect any man, woman, or child of God. A few days later, as my second volume of The New Wine was being finalized, this incredible photograph below was taken by my wife Carol Rose.

Photo: This incredible photo was taken by my wife Carol Rose in the night skies of West Michigan after I had been praying to St. Mary to ask that Lucifer/Hillel Ben Shachar/Memnoch/Satan/red dragon, the devil be bound from this earth and unable to host, possess, influence, or control any children of God. I believe this image, which appeared a few days later, is showing the fallen angel of darkness Lucifer's face in the moon. The face is to the right with a goatee, a large prominent nose, dark beady eyes, and even horns on his head. My wife and I have shown this photo to many family and friends who see the same image and agree with our assessment.

Photo: This photo was also taken by my wife Carol Rose a few frames before the previous one, and it shows the face of Lucifer/Hillel Ben Shachar/Memnoch/Satan/ red dragon/devil beginning to form in the night sky. Lucifer is also referred to as the "accuser angel" because of his tendency to try to separate you from God by accusing you before him and your fellow man.

There is something I am now going to reveal which I did not have permission from on high to do so until now. That is the scientific equation given to Albert Einstein many decades ago and also the reason why this information was given to him. That equation is $E = mc^2$, which is Energy = mass × the speed of light. The real reason this equation was given to

Albert Einstein has two purposes. The first of which is, this is the energy, mass, and speed with which an angelic spirit (think of Paxton and archangel Gabriel from vol. 2 of The New Wine departing for heaven and leaving wings in the sky behind) can move via wormholes (Einstein-Rosen bridges) across dimensions from universe to universe. This allows a spirit or angel to be in more than one dimension, more than one universe at the same time and space. This is how a spirit such as the spirit of the incarnate Son of St. Mary can be in more than one place at once. Early Catholics used to refer to this ability, which some saints were able to tap into, as "bilocation" (being in two places at once). The other reason this was given is to demonstrate the speed, energy, and mass with which the fallen angel Lucifer/Hillel Ben Shachar/Memnoch/Satan/red dragon/devil can also move from human host to human host while on the earth so we would be aware of the threat.

I would know like to share a heartbreaking story regarding $E = mc^2$ as it pertains to a young lady named Mollie Tibbetts from Iowa. Mollie was unfortunately the victim of a horrific crime after she was kidnapped and murdered by an illegal alien from Mexico. After hearing the authorities had recovered her remains, I said an entire rosary for her at St. Mary's Catholic Church in Spring Lake, Michigan. I also asked St. Mary to show me where her spirit was presently at. I was shown the Pyramids of Giza in a vision. This to me was extremely significant.

Jim Morrison and I recorded the song "The WASP (Texas Radio and the Big Beat)" while with The Doors musical group which referred to our origin and the pyramids being related to ancient half-breed aliens. He sings in this song, "We have constructed pyramids in honor of our escaping." He notes in this song that the ancient Annunaki were not always welcomed and often oppressed by humans out of fear, thus the "escaping" he refers to back to Orion's Belt.

MOLLIE TIBBETTS

Photo: The lovely Mollie Tibbetts from Brooklyn, Iowa, was a recent victim of a terrible crime in which she lost her life. After praying a full rosary, I was shown an image of the Giza Pyramids after asking St. Mary to show me where Mollie's spirit was presently at. This is an incredibly good sign as the ancient pyramids were not only communication hubs back to heaven/Eden/An located near the constellation belt of Orion, but this also a means of sending a spirit at the speed of light ($E = mc^2$) back home to our Father in heaven. Mollie is no doubt also an Anunnaki half-breed, from her dark facial features, "holy moly," and also her love of her fellow mankind and love for her family.

Photo: On the evening of January 17, 2019, minutes after finishing the section in this third volume of The New Wine honoring the life of Mollie Tibbetts from Iowa, this amazing sunset appeared in our skies near Prescott Valley, Arizona. I can't quite put words around this image it is so stunning, and I will only refer to it now as "Mollie's Sunset," in honor of the life of Mollie Tibbetts and the love she bestowed upon this world.

Photo: The image of the setting sun on January 17, 2019, very quickly morphed into what appeared as an angel on fire in flight. This amazing image showed up in our skies minutes after finishing the section in the third volume of The New Wine about Mollie Tibbetts's amazing life and her love for this world. I spoke with Mollie's family, who was very happy to include her story in this volume of The New Wine.

Not many know this fact (unless you've watched the shows Ancient Aliens or The Story of God with Morgan Freeman), but the ancient pyramids were not only power stations that allowed for heightened spiritual communication but they were also portals that allowed deceased spirits or souls safe travel back to heaven, or Eden, or as the ancients referred to it as "An," which lies in the "belt of Orion." In fact, there was a recent episode of The Story of God with Morgan Freeman where Mr. Freeman was asked to meditate on God as nuclear dye was injected into his bloodstream. His frontal lobe showed markedly more activity when he did focus on this meditation. These results were compared with a nonbeliever or atheist whose frontal lobe showed no additional activity during the same meditative exercise. This type of meditation allows us to reconnect with our place of origin (the Garden of Eden) with our alien maker (God the Father and the other kingdom). Yes, I said it here—we are creations of ancient aliens or nonhuman entities from another galaxy, and that galaxy is located in Orion's Belt.

Many people have known this for centuries, and it is a closely guarded secret by secret societies and religions. It is also a well-known fact by Lucifer/Hillel Ben Shachar/ Memnoch/Satan/red dragon/devil. In fact, if you watch any Hollywood movie made by Orion Pictures, you will see a veiled reference to this genesis in the form of the stars of the constellation Orion morphing into a wheel that becomes the letter O in Orion Pictures.

Whoever created this clever image that many of us see at the beginning of many movies knows that we are generated from Orion where the gods reside and that it is from this genesis that make all things on earth go around. Albert Einstein used meditation to tap into the Akashic records, which is essentially the spiritual vine left to us from our

Maker. This is no doubt where he retrieved the knowledge of $E = mc2$. The CIA has used similar techniques referred to as remote viewing, which is also tapping into the "universal mind" to retrieve data and knowledge not otherwise accessible. It is the same techniques I use when communing with St. Mary and the other kingdom to ascertain spiritual information and guidance/ direction and also help locate lost spirits and victims of violent crimes.

Photo: Jim Morrison's "hunter of the green vest" has wrestled before with "lions in the night," as mentioned in the lyrics of The Doors song' "The Soft Parade." I am in the middle of the photo taken in 1996 during basic combat training at Ft. Leonard Wood, Missouri, after enlisting as an army legal specialist. In the army, we were trained as "hunters" in weapons, comms, land navigation, and hand-to-hand combat.

As I mentioned in the first volume of The New Wine, I share the same middle name as Jim Morrison, same mole on my left cheek, and quite similar singing voice. I also have memories of his life I can't explain and also knew all the lyrics to The Doors' songs as a young teenager. I was recalled to active duty in fall 2003 as the United States was bombing Baghdad and was honorably discharged a week later, most likely due to the spinal cord injury I received on active duty. I believe this was divine intervention to keep me out of another unjust war for oil profit.

Photo: This incredible photo of the St. Louis Archway was snapped on our way headed west to relocate near Prescott Valley, Arizona. Notice the amazing sun's rays shooting into frame from the top right. This image was more positive confirmation of leaving our longtime home in West Michigan to live in our favorite vacation spot near the spiritually uplifting community of central Arizona.

Photo: This amazing photo showing more angel wings in the southwest skies of Sedona, Arizona, on December 20, 2018, shortly after our arrival in Arizona. This was more confirmation of protection from on high as we made our way west to our new home.

Photo: My wife Carol Rose and I, with another set of amazing fraternal twins and friends—Rachel and Callie—hiked in the red rocks of Sedona, Arizona, shortly after arriving from our cross country trip from Michigan in the winter of 2018.

DOE MOUNTAIN

Photo: The red rocks of Sedona, Arizona, are seen as we hiked up the side of Doe Mountain looking off to the west toward Bear Mountain. Carol Rose and I did this hike with our friends and fraternal twins Rachel and Callie. Sedona is not only a place of pure beauty but also a spiritual hub of unexplainable energy vortices that emanate through the rocks from deep inside the earth's crust. Many believe this is an area frequented by alien visitors from other planets.

I would like to take this time to convey an incredible story based on a communing event I completed for a dear friend of mine named Jennifer Duncan from Indiana.

Jennifer heard some of my stories from my other volumes of The New Wine and asked if I could find out from St. Mary where her father was presently at. Her father, a man named David Crawford, had passed away in the midinettes after battling years of addiction. When I asked my good friend Jen if she believed he was not in a good place because of how he died, she replied yes. After a full rosary a day later, I asked St. Mary if I could commune with Jen's deceased father David. Prior to this, I knew absolutely nothing about her father except for the way in which he died more than twenty years prior.

While at St. Mary's Catholic Church in Spring Lake, Michigan, I was hit immediately with a very fast-moving and highly intelligent male spirit. This man showed me images of different colored Chevrolet Corvettes driving around a race track that I presumed to be at the Indianapolis 500 Race. He was showing me he can attend the Indy 500 as an audience member and also drive any color, make, and model Corvette around the same track when no one is around. David then showed me a young girl with ponytails who I presumed to be my friend Jennifer at a younger age. She was blowing out candles on a chocolate birthday cake. David also made it quite clear that he found it amusing that his daughter Jennifer didn't think she could commune with spirits like I can, and he told me she had this ability but just has never used it.

As I relayed this information to my friend Jen, she stated, "That's my dad. He used to drive only Corvettes and attended the Indy 500 every year, and when I was really young, he bought me chocolate cake for my birthday." It seems I was definitely in contact with her father's spirit. Jennifer still doesn't believe she can commune with the other side, but David and I know that she can. It also goes to show you that we can never judge another person's spiritual journey, no matter what obstacles they may have struggled with in life. It is not our job to do so.

David Crawford

Photo: David Crawford from Indianapolis, the father of my very good friend named Jennifer Duncan, shown here many years ago in the early nineties. I was able to spiritually commune with him after saying a rosary at church in fall 2018. The information I gave Jennifer confirmed it was her father who I had, in fact, contacted.

He was living the "high life in the afterlife," driving Corvettes at the Indy 500 and still making birthday cakes for his daughter Jennifer.

Photo: Here is my very good friend Jennifer Duncan from Westfield, Indiana, at a young age showing the chocolate birthday cake her father David would buy for her every birthday.

Shortly before moving out west to Arizona, my good friend Jennifer Duncan from Indiana became really ill with an upper respiratory infection. I had been waking up almost every night around this time at exactly three o'clock in the morning, which many believe to be the witching hour. I told my local parish priest Father Dave whom I believed I would be under enormous spiritual attack until The New Wine Volume 2 was finally published and released because I had directly called out Lucifer in that volume.

On the same day my friend Jennifer became sick, I woke up in the middle of the night very restless. I decided to go in the middle of the night to a nearby statue of St. Mary holding her fallen Son and say a full rosary asking for healing for my friend

Jennifer and also to be able to sleep peacefully. As I was driving back home, I saw a very large male deer with multiple points sitting motionless in a neighbor's yard. He stared right at me before running off. Very soon I fell into a deep sleep then texted my friend Jennifer in the morning to relay this information and let her know I had prayed for her to be healed. Jennifer stated she felt almost completely better and not as sick as the day before.

Photo: St. Mary holding a fallen Jesus in front of St. Mary's Catholic Church in Spring Lake, Michigan. This is the very statue I prayed at in the middle of the night for healing for my friend Jennifer Duncan from Indiana and for me to be able to sleep peacefully at night until the publication of The New Wine Volume 2 meant to help bind "lions in the night" from this earth.

Photo: A deer in similar size and number of points hit by my car in October 2018. An almost exact size male deer with similar number of points appeared on a neighbor's lawn after driving home in the middle of the night later in the fall after saying a full rosary for healing for my friend Jennifer and for protection for us all from the "lions in the night."

On Christmas Day, December 25, 2018, my wife Carol Rose and I attended a Spanish Catholic Mass at Sacred Heart Catholic Church in Prescott, Arizona. After the Mass, my wife had a conversation with the Mexican American priest stating that she felt frustrated because she didn't understand the language of the Mass as it was said in Spanish. The priest jokingly and kindly replied that Christianity is the universal word—that is, for everyone regardless of their heritage. I found that statement profoundly accurate and insightful. While we were at the beautiful Catholic church, I said an entire rosary for another dear friend who was facing a medical crisis and might end up losing her finger

due to a lifelong infectious process and ulceration on her hand. On our way back home to Prescott Valley, Arizona, my wife and I stopped by to take a few photos with some local black Angus cows. As we were doing this, the most amazing image of the sunrays shooting down from clouds above was caught by my cell phone's camera.

Photo: An amazing image of the sun shooting its healing rays down from the other kingdom on high after celebrating a Catholic Mass on Christmas Day and praying for a dear friend who had a medical crisis.

On the morning of December 27, 2018, after finishing a social media conversation with a new angelic friend who expressed interest in helping to promote my book/screenplay The New Wine, the following sunrise appeared over southwest skies of Arizona appearing as a fire in the sky.

Photo: An amazing sunrise over the southwestern skies of central Arizona showing the sky figuratively on fire in January 2019. No doubt a view from our Mother St. Mary after having a very positive conversation with a new friend regarding The New Wine book/screenplay.

ANUNNAKI ANGELS HALF-HUMAN

    I want to take a moment to identify more half-breeds. As I mentioned in The New Wine Volume 2, there are quite a few half-human, half-Anunnaki angels that have landed in the film and music industries. After a review of some more Hollywood movies and music videos, I would have to also add Angelina Jolie, Ashley Judd, Jill Hennessy, Sandra Bullock, Natalie Portman, Tom Selleck, Brooke Fraser, Giovanni Ribisi, Naomi Watts, Rose Byrne, Liv Tyler, Patrick Swayze, Matthew Broderick, Russell Crowe, Mick Jagger, Jeff and Beau Bridges, Kevin Kline, Chevy Chase, Topher Grace, Natalie Imbruglia, Katie Holmes, Geena Davis, Ewan McGregor, James Marsden, Kyle Chandler, Dylan Minnette, Robert Downey Jr., Johnny Depp, Bruce Willis, Charlie Sheen, Cate Blanchett, Burt Reynolds, Linda Ronstadt, Robin Williams, Daniel Day Lewis, Jeff Goldblum, Meg Tilly, Emmy Rossum, Susan Sarandon, Mark Wahlberg, Martin Sheen, Ben Stiller, Mark Ruffalo, Henry Thomas, Natalie Merchant, Linda Hamilton, Eliza Dushku, Martina McBride, Maynard James Keenan, Elizabeth Reaser, Mark Hamill, Carrie Fisher, Carrie-Ann Moss, Seth Rogen, Harrison Ford, Kurt Russell, Sylvester Stallone, George Michael, Lauren Daigle, Kirk Hammett, Billy Joel, Dave Grohl, Johnette Napolitano, Karen Carpenter, Adrien Brody, Sarah McLachlan, Dolores O'Riordan, Mickey Rourke, Brad Pitt, Bradley Cooper, Brad Davis, Julia Roberts, Kevin Bacon, Kyra Sedgwick, Mel Gibson, George Clooney, Tom Hanks, Ryan Bingham, Tom Berenger, Leonardo DiCaprio, Adam Scott, Adam Driver, Michelle Pfeiffer, Jake and Maggie Gyllenhaal, Kirk and Michael Douglas, Stanley Kubrick, Jessica Chastain, Kim Cattrall, Kate Capshaw, Harley Jane Kozak, Heath Ledger, Anne Hathaway, Jennifer Garner, Winona Ryder, Keira Knightley, Rachel McAdams, Daisy Ridley, Jessica Biel, Ellen Page, Jami Gertz, Shia LaBeouf, Linda Carter, Matthew Perry, Carly Simon, Kim Raver, Kate and Rooney Mara, Courtney Cox, Cristin Milioti, Jeanne Tripplehorn, Jason Lee, Jason Schwartzman, Andy Garcia, Kevin Pollak, Christian Slater, River and Joaquin Phoenix, Madonna, Amanda Peet, Ashton Kutcher, Mila Kunis, Vince Vaughn, Jon Favreau, Abbie Cornish, Catherine Zeta-Jones, Jim Carrey, Cameron Diaz, Alec, William, Billy, and Stephen Baldwin, Tom Morello, Eric Bana, Chris Pine, Minnie Driver, Chris Hemsworth, Elsa Pataky, John Travolta, Kelly Preston, Juliette Lewis, Michelle Williams, Michael Fassbender, Hilary Swank, Jim and John Belushi, Luke and Owen Wilson, Josh Hartnett, Sam

Rockwell, Lizzy Kaplan, Mia Sara, Angie Harmon, Anthony Kiedis, Neil Diamond, Kurt Cobain, Jennifer Esposito, Blake Lively, Elizabeth Perkins, Margaret Colin, Kate Jackson, Jaclyn Smith, Gordon Sumner (Sting), Freddie Mercury, Susanna Hoffs, Don Henley, Michael Hutchence (whom I firmly believe was actually St. Michael the Archangel incarnate), Aaron Sorkin, Kate Winslet, Ryan Gosling, Ryan Reynolds, Shannon Hoon, Garth Brooks, Clint Black, Brit Marling, Chris Evans, Luke Perry, John Krasinski, Hugh Grant, Aaron Eckhart, Emily Blunt, Sarah Fay Wright Olsen, Scott Stapp, Sully Erna, John Lennon, Meg Ryan, Celine Dion, Polly Samson, David Gilmour (whose prophecy in the Pink Floyd song "Brain Damage / Eclipse" has since come true), Dave Matthews, Aja Volkman, Gary Rossington, Stephanie Germanotta (Lady Gaga), Ronnie and Johnny Van Zant, Ray Manzarek, Johnny Cash, Waylon Jennings, Ann Wilson, and a new name Aydan Schlaffman, who, although still finishing high school, is a member of what I believe will be a jam band who will eventually surpass The Doors called Obscure Identity. I've spoken on the phone with Aydan (whose first name means both "from the moon" and also "little fire"), and he is hugely influenced by Jim Morrison. Aydan is also the keyboardist for his band (who when I hear him play, I hear Ray Manzarek).

"Beautiful Swan" and "Endless Life"

As I watched you glide over the field,

I knew you were the one

Take me to your heart,

And let's slip into love.

Every night you've been haunting my dreams,

You appear in the bliss

Your eyes fire, hair water

I need your care.

Keep the monster under quarantine,

Unwanted fear is here,

Down whispering roads,

Worlds are filled with the unknown.

Eyes are lies,

Filled with pain

From the other ones.

Elaborate plans,

Distinguished minds.

As you levitate,

My heart is filled with darkness.

Sweeping through the halls,

I need your light,

My gracious one,

I need to see you again.

Beautiful Swan,

If we die together,

It'll be okay.

We'll fall forever and never wake.

The lights are out,

The ship is boarding,

Take my hand,

And we will go,

And never come back.

Endless Life

Endless life

Endless life

Endless life

My fear would be

Endless life

Endless life

Endless life

The world is untrue

Last breath will be

Quick and concealed

Soul will vanish

Never to heal

Last sight will be

Filled with thought

Mind will forget

All that was taught

Rotting corpse lay

Deep in the ground

A waste of time to be

Unsafe and unsound

To be patient

The gift has arrived

The gift to make sure

Your name has survived

Endless life

Endless life

Endless life

My fear would be

Endless life

Endless life

Endless life

The world is untrue

Life's piano

Divine and so real

Place a flower

Crying to kneel

Surviving

You only suffice

The grass is so cold

The reason of ice

Dead bolt window

Plastered caress

Plaguing evening

I lie and confess

Unearthly presence

Thrown into shade

Shadows walking

Where we played

Fade to white

Doubting these

Newborn tears

Weak today

Facing your fears

Until there's

Nothing to slay

Cradle me

I'm all alone

In a room full of friends

Wicked laugh

Your mind intends

To like despair

Cut to black

Wicked 'shroom

Dancing on dirt

Doctor Danger

Looming to flirt

He takes his hand

And he searches for thrill

Desperate dreaming

Dresses to kill

Watching over

Thinking of love

Seems I missed out

On some kind of glove

A glove to fit me

Right into place

I hate to scream it but

"Oh, my poor face!"

Endless life,

Endless life

Endless life,

My fear would be

Endless life,

Endless life

Endless life,

The world is untrue

—Aydan Schlaffman

What's fascinating about Aydan's poem "Beautiful Swan" is that there is an actual Catholic "Order of The Swan" which is a Marian Catholic Order and also, he refers to "worlds" in this poem. This is significant because St. Mary in her apparitions has spoken of numerous worlds, cosmos, galaxies, and the universe as a multiverse with other civilizations. When I spoke live with Aydan, he told me an amazing story that I believe is proof he can host and channel Jim Morrison as well. He told me that one time he was driving with his father in his car and told him to turn the radio channel to another radio channel because he knew that "Riders on the Storm" by The Doors was playing.

This is clearly a case of Jim influencing a young artist in a profoundly creative way.

Photo: Here are the young rockers of Obscure Identity, the next new great jam band led by young Aydan Schlaffman on keyboards who is yet another incarnation of Dionysus—a.k.a., Jim Morrison—and part of the scattered Son of St. Mary.

The individuals mentioned above I would add now to the list of half-breeds that I revealed in the second volume of The New Wine. Also, I would definitely have to add Val Kilmer to the list as well whom I met for the first time recently after his Citizen

Twain show. His portrayal of me and Jim in Oliver Stone's movie The Doors should have garnered him an Oscar nomination. The performance was brilliant and spot on.

I was fortunate enough to meet him recently and view his amazing portrayal of Mark Twain in Citizen Twain, a one-man show. Although not everything in his portrayal of Jim was accurate, Val captured many positive nuances of Jim's personality that

were very accurate. What's quite fascinating is one could almost write an entire book on Anunnaki in modern film, as many of these actors and actresses have not only been in many movies together, but some of them also married each other and have had children that would also be half-breeds.

These half-breed individuals would also have a very strong spiritual connection to the other kingdom of angels and saints and would also have abilities that would be defined by others as supernatural, if properly unlocked. As I also mentioned before, I am certain there are others, some of who may not be actively working in the film and music industries like myself but would nevertheless have inherent spiritual abilities that would super cede the normal parameters of what we would define as human. The primary identifying features of these individuals would be dark or tanned facial features with the presence of moles on the face (holy moly).

On January 5, 2019, the exact day of my own earth father Bill's sixty-ninth birthday, my wife Carol and I were hiking around noon at Thumb Butte near Prescott, Arizona, as I prayed for St. Mary to once again send down the sun's healing rays to all of God's children from the other kingdom. What happened next was simply indescribable.

Within minutes, a 6.1 magnitude earthquake struck Alaska, and thirty minutes later, a 6.8 magnitude earthquake struck Brazil around the exact time I took the photo below showing multiple sunrays streaking down from the other kingdom across Thumb Butte near Prescott, Arizona.

Photo: St. Mary's "Sun's Rays," a hike on January 5, 2019, the exact date of my earth father Bill's sixty-ninth birthday showing scattered multicolored rays of sunlight shooting down from heaven/Eden/An at around noon—the same time when two major earthquakes struck both

Alaska and Brazil. The magnitudes of the earthquakes were a magnitude 6.1 in Alaska and 6.8 in Brazil. If you add those numbers, you get 6.9 on my father's sixty-ninth birthday. When I asked St. Mary if this was deliberate, she stated that those were my father's "birthday quakes."

Photo: Matthew Douglas Pinard (The New Wine) hiking with wife Carol Rose Kloss (The New Rose) near Thumb Butte in Prescott, Arizona, on my father Bill's sixty-ninth birthday on January 5, 2019. I always found it amusing that technically I am older than my own father. The sun's healing rays are shining down from Heaven/ Eden/An from behind us.

    I want to now tell the story of an amazingly strong young lady named Jayme Closs from Wisconsin. Jayme was kidnapped around Christmas time this past year of 2018 after an intruder shot and killed her parents. I became aware of the case only after I received an intuition one morning from St. Mary after saying an entire rosary to show me what she wanted me to see next. After reading of Jayme's tragic family story online,

I had a few distinct images that I was given from St. Mary that I believed might help authorities locate her. The first image was an image of a local county fair and many people walking around the fair. The second image was of a dark-colored SUV driving through a fast-food drive-through. This particular image came to me after I asked St. Mary to be able to see through Jayme's eyes. It was if I were in the back seat of this vehicle and I could see the vehicle driving through the fast-food restaurant. I had the distinct impression that Jayme was still alive. I immediately called the tip line from Wisconsin and gave them these details. A day later, a special agent from the FBI in Minnesota called me to follow up. I explained to him my ability to see things some people would not normally be able to see with their mind's eye.

After taking my notes, I let him know that I looked up online and saw that there had been a local county fair (unknown to me at the time) the previous fall in this area. In any event, I prayed every day a full rosary for the safe return of Jayme as I also asked for St. Mary to wrap Jayme in Archangel Gabriel's wings for protection. I also implored the spiritual abilities of my wife whose last name is also "Kloss."

While at St. Patrick's Catholic Church, I asked St. Mary to show Carol Kloss where Jayme Closs was currently at. Immediately Carol received an image of a hunting cabin in the middle of the woods. I also received an image of what appeared to me as a hunting cabin surrounded by woods. We immediately called this tip into the tip line and said more prayers for the safe return of Jayme Closs to her family. The area in which Jayme was eventually found was a rural area in central Wisconsin in a neighborhood with cabinlike homes surrounded by woods.

A similar experience of this kind of clairvoyant viewing occurred to me about a year before Jayme Closs's disappearance and recovery. I ended up calling an FBI tip line after stumbling across a flyer near a rest area seeking information and tips regarding the very disturbing murder of two local Indiana sisters Abby and Libby near Delphi, Indiana. The murder was shocking in that one of the girls had the incredible courage to videotape the murderer as he approached the girls. The man had a beard, sunglasses, and a dark coat. The video is extremely disturbing as you can hear the man tell the girls to meet him down near the river.

After a full rosary at St. Mary's Catholic Church in Spring Lake, Michigan, I called the tip line because I distinctly saw the inside of a home with a red brick fireplace and what appeared to me as a white cutty ship on top of the mantle of the fireplace. I called the authorities and stated I believed that these items would be found in the suspect's home. I have not heard whether this information proved to be true, but I do know as of this date there has been no arrests in this case.

Photo: This stock photo of a hunting cabin near woods looks very similar to the same kind of cabin that actually exists in the neighborhood of where Jayme Closs was eventually found alive in central Wisconsin. This image of a cabin was given to both my wife and I as we prayed for Jayme's safe return to her family.

JAYME CLOSS

Photo: An undated photo of the amazing Jayme Closs from Wisconsin who was abducted after her parents were murdered and was recently found alive after major search efforts by local authorities and the FBI. On January 10, 2019, local authorities of the Baron County Sheriff's Office in Wisconsin notified they had located Jayme Closs alive and had taken her abductor into custody. All our prayers for JC's safe return had been answered.

Photo: An incredibly beautiful sunset near my new hometown of Prescott Valley, Arizona, on January 10, 2019. I knew after looking up at this in the sky that the world would be receiving some good news very soon. Within hours, local authorities announced the safe return of Jayme Closs to her family in Wisconsin.

    The morning before the world knew that Jayme Closs would escape and be found alive, I randomly decided to attend a local mass at St. Germaine Catholic Church in Prescott Valley, Arizona. St. Germaine was a French Catholic saint born in 1579 who suffered horrific abuses as a child and who showed great kindness and mercy to local beggars. Local legend has it that when St. Germaine died, a celestial body of angels and saints was seen by travelers in remote areas of the forest surrounded by a blinding light; and after her death, her body took on a beautiful form and did not decay. As I was seated in a pew, an older Asian woman took my hand out of the blue as we said prayers and then handed me the following prayer card of the Taxiarch Angel St. Michael.

She had no idea who I was or what my own personal journey was. She also had no idea I had just published a book naming Lucifer/Hillel Ben Shachar/Memnoch/Satan/ red dragon/devil as the fallen entity currently enacting chaos on the world or that I had been also praying for the safe return of Jayme Closs to her family.

Photo: St. Michael the Taxiarch Angel in battle against Lucifer and all his "lions of the night." This prayer card was handed to me the morning of Jayme Closs's escape from her abductor in rural Wisconsin. St. Michael is known as the "Taxiarch Angel,"

which translates to "brigadier"—as in, a military brigadier general. He is the chief adversary of Lucifer/Hillel Ben Shachar/Memnoch/Satan/red dragon/devil.

My response to this kind woman who gave me the St. Michael prayer card was to show her my photo of St. Gabriel's wings that appeared to us at young Paxton Elkins's funeral in the second volume of The New Wine, Peace Town.

ARCHANGEL GABRIEL'S FOLDED WINGS

Photo: Archangel Gabriel's folded wings that appeared in the sky over northern Indiana at the gravesite of young Paxton Elkins after his untimely death in fall 2017 following his courageous battle with terminal brain cancer.

Photo: This amazing sunset appeared on May 26, 2017, off the coast of Grand Haven, Michigan. While this photo is included in The New Wine Volume 2: Peace Town, I did not recognize the significance of it until I checked the date. May 26, 2009, was the date of Paxton Elkins's birth. This amazing view of the new sun setting appeared on Paxton's eighth birthday as he courageously battled terminal brain cancer.

Photo: Young Paxton Elkins earned his permanent wings after his battle with terminal brain cancer. There is no doubt in my mind he and Archangels Gabriel and Michael were protecting Jayme Closs following her abduction and the murder of her parents in central Wisconsin in late 2018.

The morning after Jayme Closs was found alive in rural Wisconsin, I stopped by Sacred Heart Catholic Church in Prescott, Arizona, to thank my mother St. Mary for answering all of our prayers for this courageous young girl's return home safely to her family. As I sat and recited an entire rosary, the sun began to shine directly through the stained-glass window in the church through St. Mary's sacred heart.

Photo: The sun shining brightly through the stained-glass sacred heart of St. Mary at Sacred Heart Catholic Church in Prescott, Arizona, the morning of January 11, 2019—a day after the world learned young Jayme Closs had escaped from her abductor. I want to point out something quite profound that the artist of this stain glass window no doubt deliberately included in this artwork. There are seven stars surrounding St. Mary in this stained-glass window. As we know seven is a biblically significant and mystical number that trumps the demonic number of six.

Photo: The morning after I received my proof books of The New Wine Volume 2 in mid-January 2019 for review, this sunrise appeared near our new home of Prescott Valley, Arizona. The sunrise is almost identical to the one we saw a few weeks earlier after our arrival in Arizona from Michigan on the morning of December 27, 2018.

Photo: On the early morning of January 16, 2019, the day I would receive proof copies of my second book dedicated to the memory of young Paxton Elkins from Portage, Indiana, this incredible mystic mountain mist appeared before dawn near our new home in Prescott Valley, Arizona. It is one of the most alluring images I've ever seen in nature. The date was remarkable because it represented exactly fifteen months to the day since Paxton's passing from this earth. Fifteen months is also the amount of time he lived following his diagnosis for DIPG brain cancer.

    On the morning of January 16, 2019, as I said a full rosary of prayers to St. Mary in remembrance of the life of young Paxton Elkins, I asked her to "bring fire from the earth" so the world will never forget his sacrifice and also so the world will embrace our two keys of "Be Love" and "Believe." The next day, another dormant volcano erupted in southern Japan.

Photo: A volcano erupts in southern Japan on January 17, 2019, one day after I asked St. Mary to "bring fire from the earth" in remembrance of the sacrifice of young Paxton Elkins and for the world to embrace our two keys of "Be Love" and "Believe" and disarm all weapons of mass destruction.

Photo: On the morning of January 18, 2019, my wife Carol Rose (The New Rose, as introduced in the first volume of The New Wine) took this amazing photograph near our home in Prescott Valley, Arizona. There are two large sunrays pointing to heaven and earth and a very peculiar green orb or object to the top left of the frame.

Photo: I found this photograph online taken by an overseas photographer of a similar green looking object to the left of the sun. Many have theorized this is the mythical planet Nibiru or one of its moons. The ancient Sumerians referred to Nibiru as the "Red Dragon" and also the "destroyer of worlds" crossing our solar system every 3,600 years, brining major earthquakes, volcanoes, tsunamis, and floods.

Photo: My wife and I blew up another photo of this green object and found an odd human-type figure with its arms outstretched within it. It was unusual and worth including in this book. We cannot explain the above image taken in the fall of 2018 at all. What I will include with this image is a passage of prophecy from Matthew 24:33, and that passage states, "So likewise ye, when ye shall see all these things, know that it [the end] is near, even at the doors" (KJV). Yes, this passage that predicts the second coming of Christ is also a veiled reference to my half-brother James and my band called The Doors and the prophetic song "The End."

Photo: The early morning of January 21, 2019, following the super blood wolf moon of 2019, this amazing photo shows the new moon casting light rays across the dark skies, and you can see more multicolored orbs to the right as have appeared in photos of the sun in my previous volumes of The New Wine. The amazing photo also shows what appears to be angel wings emanating from the moon.

Photo: Another shot of the new moon the morning of January 21, 2019, near St. Germaine Catholic Church in Prescott Valley, Arizona, showing amazing rays of light streaking across the morning skies.

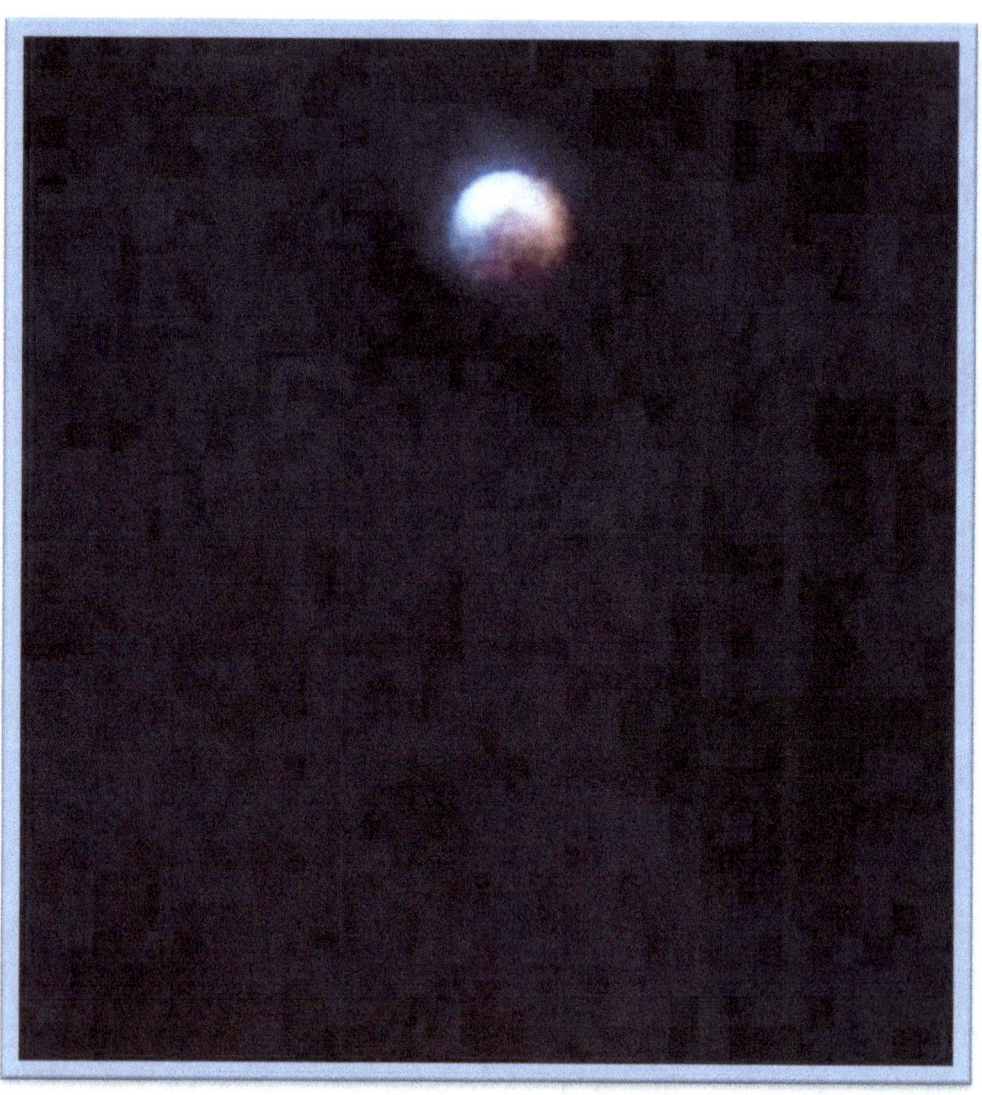

Photo: Another amazing photo of the super blood wolf moon of January 21, 2019, as taken by my "fraternal twin" sister, Alanis Morisette, also born in 1974.

Photo: The morning of January 21, 2019, after our super blood wolf moon, this sunrise appeared in Prescott Valley, Arizona, firing golden sun rays across the earth.

Photo: The morning of January 21, 2019, the super blood wolf moon near Prescott Valley, Arizona.

"BE LOVE" AND "BELIEVE"

Photo: Another amazing sunrise the morning of January 23, 2019, after a full rosary at St. Germaine's Catholic Church in Prescott Valley, Arizona. My prayers were focused on the acceptance of our two keys of "Be Love" and "Believe" to be embraced by all of mankind.

    I want to take a moment to discuss the subtitle of The New Wine Volume 3 and explain why "The Veil Rent" was chosen as a title for this volume. The definition of veil is a "piece of see-through fabric meant to cover something (in religious circles the face)." The definition of rent means to "pay someone for use of something." The spiritual definitions of both these words used in concert have connotations to both St.

Mary and her incarnate sons. (Yes, there have been now three.) Earlier in this volume, I showed another photograph of a veiled woman's face clothed with the sun. This woman is St. Mary, and she is wearing a veil to show the world her role and place in the Holy Trinity.

"The Veil Rent," which is the title of this book, refers to the event following the crucifixion of Jesus Christ on the cross. As he bowed his head and said "It is finished," an earthquake struck and the veil inside the temple in Jerusalem was torn in two, or "rent." This event was referred to as the "veil being rent," which is interesting because it can also be translated as "the debt has been paid." As it pertains to the message of this third volume of The New Wine, when referring to the "veil," we not only are referencing St. Mary's headdress; we are also referring to each and every human being's identity within Christ in terms of your life being a unique mystery in and of itself.

Let me explain further. Each of us was given a name at birth; for some of us, that name may have held special meaning to our parents or they may have been moved by the Holy Spirit to choose that name. That certainly is what I believe was the case with young Paxton Elkins and his first name translating to "peace town" as described in The New Wine Volume 2: Peace Town. Paxton's birth, life, and even death was all mapped out by our Creator well in advance; and he was given a name to help us identify his role in this world, which, in my opinion, is bringing us all peace. Knowing now that each and every one of us has a special place in God's other kingdom, would that better inform you how to live your life? That is to say, if you knew you had a special purpose from St. Mary and her incarnate "scattered son," would you not do everything within your power to uncover what that special mission is, especially if fulfilling that mission meant eternal life?

Photo: "The New Rose," my wife Carol Rose, at Bearizona Animal Park near Williams, Arizona, on February 9, 2019. An incredible ray of light is captured shining down from the other kingdom above.

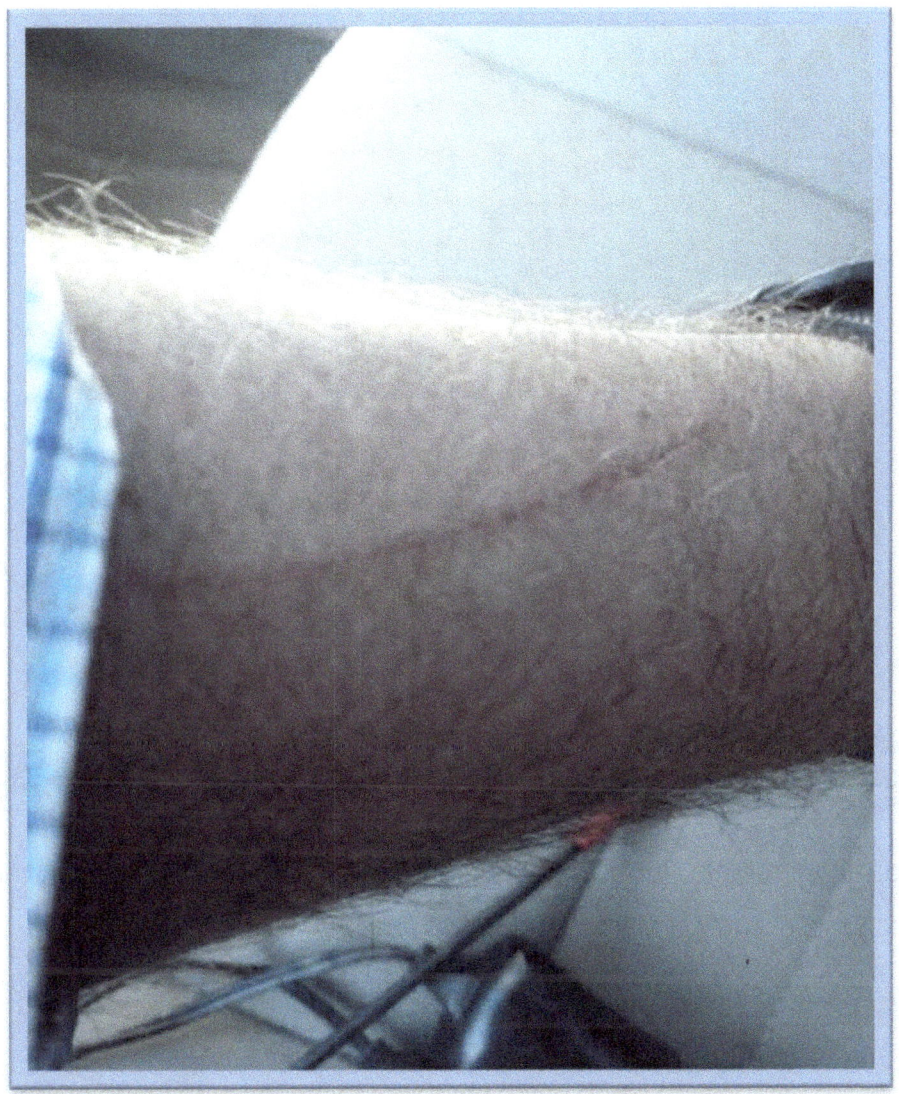

Photo: On the morning of February 11, 2019, I woke up with a very mysterious long red scratch on my arm that was not there the previous night. Considering my dogs slept in the other room that night, I can only categorize this mark as a supernatural, unexplained phenomenon. I do believe this is further proof we are definitively in the Book of Revelations and the apocalypse. As I stated in The New Wine Volume 2, apocalypse also translates to "new beginning."

Photo: An incredible rainbow-looking sunset near Prescott, Arizona, the evening of February 11, 2019, taken by my wife, Carol Rose.

Photo: The sunrise the morning of February 15, 2019, as I headed toward Santa Barbara, California, to visit friends.

PEACE TOWN

Photo: A painting inside the Old Mission in Santa Barbara, California. I've included this image because it is the first depiction, I've ever seen of three sons of Mary sitting behind her placing a crown upon her head. This seems a highly prophetic image as The New Wine Volume 1 presents the proposition that St. Mary has had three incarnate sons in the last two thousand years. I also referred to this in The New Wine Volume 2: Peace Town as the spiritual phenomenon known as "son stacking."

The image also depicts a crowing of St. Mary as she would receive her full status as being fully "Deus" and now part of the Holy Trinity, should her "son stacking" mission prove to be successful. As I wrote in The New Wine Volume 1 in my continuation of the poem "An American Prayer," "This other Kingdom is by far the best, the feast of friends now in he who is three all for our mother to see." Jim and I sang about this in The Doors' song "Waiting for the Sun" with the lyrics, "Sun, sun, sun." I would also be remiss here if I did not mention my own earth mother who gave birth to the third son—her name is Barbara Jean Pinard, born in 1947. (Yes, I am older than my own earth mother too.) The Old Mission at Santa Barbara is named after Saint Barbara and founded by Franciscans in 1786. I personally contacted the Old Mission at Santa Barbara to inquire as the genesis of this painting. The official response was that the three sons above St. Mary in this painting were intended to represent the Father, the Son, and the Holy Spirit; and all intended to look the same in appearance. The Old Mission stated this painting was most likely a Miguel Cabrera painting and there were likely several painters of this mural. This is specifically how St. Mary likes to work. She likes to inspire multiple artists to create pieces of art, poetry, and musical lyrics with definitively with more than one possible meaning within those works.

Jim Morrison inherently understood this sacred mystery of the other kingdom and how the two kingdoms were truly connected and as such purposefully intended multiple meanings with his lyrics and poetry. My personal belief is this painter—or, rather, painters—of this mural not only intended to represent the Holy Trinity here but also, subconsciously were prophesying through the Holy Spirit that, as of the publication date of The New Wine, there would be three incarnate sons of St. Mary since the crucifixion and pending apocalypse. All three, like the figures above, would be intricately connected through space and time as well as spiritually conjoined.

Photo: An amazing sunset off the coast of Santa Barbara, California, on February 16, 2019, after attending a memorial service of a friend of a friend who passed away very suddenly in January. This sunset appeared a day after intense rain and clouds, which is highly abnormal for even Southern California. I had prayed a full rosary earlier in the day at the Old Mission in Santa Barbara for St. Mary to enter this dearly departed friend of a friend into the other kingdom without delay.

Photo: This incredible image was taken by my wife Carol Rose as she was driving near the Dells in Prescott, Arizona, on February 23, 2019. This image came after two straight days of blizzard like conditions that delivered the most snowfall in the entire history of northern Arizona. While Carol saw an angel in flight looking backward with its right arm pointing to the ground, I saw the eye of Horus in the center with an all-seeing eye staring straight ahead. In recent days, I had been praying for St. Mary to give me more signs from the skies for the third volume of The New Wine.

Photo: This incredible image of an orb appearing as a "blue eye" was taken by my wife Carol Rose, shortly after the appearance of the strange cloud pattern on February 23, 2019. What's interesting to me is that this orb is very similar to the ones taken by my own camera, only it is of a different color. The orbs I had taken were red in appearance and described by friends as simply lens flares. I enclosed these images in the first two volumes of The New Wine. This photo was taken by my wife Carol with her camera while I was not with her. It appears to me as the blue eye of Horus enclosed by a purple haze. The eye of Horus is an ancient Egyptian sign of protection, royal power, and good health and a sign that God is with us.

Photo: Another angelic-looking cloud formation with wings spread on March 1, 2019, while hiking in Sedona, Arizona. That same morning, I had attended a Catholic Mass at St. Germaine Catholic Church in Prescott Valley, Arizona, where we said prayers to Taxiarch Angel St. Michael for protection from Lucifer and his "lions of the night." I prayed for more signs in the skies for our third volume of The New Wine.

Photo: Yet another amazing angel cloud formation near Sedona, Arizona, on March 1, 2019, after praying earlier in the day for Taxiarch Angel St. Michael to show us his wings as we hiked near the Red Rock National Forest. I can't profess to say whether these are Michael's wings or not, but this photo is breathtakingly beautiful.

Photo: An incredibly beautiful and mysterious photo of our new sun taken right around 3:00 p.m. in the skies above Sedona, Arizona, on March 1, 2019, while hiking. There is yet another very interesting bluish-green orb present to the top right and angelic rainbow-colored wings spreading out.

Photo: Another amazing sunset view over the skies near Sedona, Arizona, on March 1, 2019, showing a very odd green, circular object to the top left of the sky that also appears to once again be partially covered by clouds. I have no explanation for what this object could be.

Photo: Another amazing view of the new sun near in the skies above Sedona, Arizona, on March 1, 2019, as my wife and I hiked near the Red Rocks. This photo was taken with her camera and shows yet another green orblike object in the middle of the frame. You can see another hiker to the left standing in the frame for reference.

MISSING

Photo: A missing child flyer at a local Walgreens Pharmacy in Prescott, Arizona, for fifteen-year-old Rilee Dennis who disappeared a day after my forty-fifth birthday on February 27, 2019. I spoke with his grandmother Sheila who said his mother was very distraught and believed in her heart that her son Rilee had passed away. Sheila accepted any kind of clairvoyant assistance I could give the family.

After saying a full rosary for Rilee, I received the word mallard, which, at this date and time, doesn't make any sense to any of us. I believe it will have meaning once the authorities uncover what happened to this kind young man. I also stated I did not believe he had passed away. It is interesting. After saying my usual rosary at Sacred Heart Catholic Church in Prescott Valley, Arizona, on Saturday, on March 2, 2019, I decided to visit this particular Walgreens for reasons unknown at the time and stumbled across the flyer.

Photo: This incredible image of an angel-like cloud formation appeared in the skies above Prescott Valley, Arizona, on March 3, 2019, after attending a local mass at Sacred Heart Catholic Church in Prescott, Arizona, and saying prayers of deliverance for fifteen-year-old Rilee Dennis for his safe return to his family. I prayed at church for St. Michael and St. Gabriel to wrap their wings safely around Rilee Dennis until his safe return to this family, and this image appeared shortly after. If I had to guess, this could very well be St. Michael's wing of protection from on high.

Photo: In the photo, another angelic winged cloud formation above the skies near Prescott Valley, Arizona, on March 3, 2019, after praying at a local Catholic Church for the safe return of Rilee Dennis to his family and for world peace.

Photo: A third beautiful angel wing cloud formation in the skies above Prescott Valley, Arizona, on March 3, 2019, after attending a local Catholic Mass and saying prayers for the safe return of fifteen-year-old Rilee Dennis to his family and for world peace. If you look closely enough in the middle of the angel wing, there appears to be a smaller figure that appears to be walking to the left along the bottom wing.

Photo: A close-up zoom-in of the figure appearing to walk on the clouds above. I showed this image to Rilee Dennis's grandmother Sheila, and she said, "That's our boy walking with the angels." My prayers earlier in the day while at Sacred Heart Catholic Church in Prescott, Arizona, near where Rilee had gone missing the week before had focused on his safe return to his family and also for St. Michael and St. Gabriel to wrap Rilee safely in their wings as protection from this darkness that has befallen his family.

Photo: Another amazing angel cloud formation above the skies near Prescott Valley, Arizona, on March 3, 2019. I definitely see a face with two eyes and two horns from its head near the top middle.

Photo: A close-up of the previous image showing what I would definitively call a mask or face to the right with eyes, nose, mouth, and horns protruding from its head but also with definitive wings in flight, taken on March 3, 2019. This image is spiritually ironic, in my opinion. This could be both an angel and/or demon, which would lend to spiritual confusion which is one of the hallmarks of Lucifer/Hillel Ben Shachar/Memnoch/Satan/red dragon/devil's tactics to keep the children spiritually anesthetized and in the night.

Photo: An amazing shot of the new sun over the skies of Phoenix, Arizona, taken on March 3, 2019, by my wife Carol Rose as she hiked with a friend. Notice how the sun's rays form an almost-perfect Christian cross, and once again there is a blue-green object or orb seen in the frame.

Photo: The sunrise on March 6, 2019, a day after meeting the family of missing teen Rilee Dennis in Prescott, Arizona, who were very appreciative of my efforts to try to help locate him using the only clue I've been given to date, which was the word mallard.

I did find a neighborhood where he had been recently spotted in a neighboring town with a street named Mallard that had a nearby Christian ministry that has been known to take in teen boys on the run. Hopefully, this clue will be a turning point in this case.

Photo: While saying a full rosary for any clues on the whereabouts of local missing teen Rilee Dennis in Prescott, Arizona, I was given this image of a mallard duck.

The image didn't make any sense to me at first until I gave this word to his Rilee's grandmother Sheila who found that a nearby town where Rilee was last spotted had a Mallard Drive in it.

Photo: This is Mallard Drive in Prescott Valley, Arizona, not far from where local teen Rilee Dennis went missing on February 27, 2019. I found this street after a vision given to me by St. Mary of a mallard duck. We are all praying for the safe return of Rilee Dennis to his family.

Update: I am extremely excited to report that Rilee Dennis was found safe and alive at a fast-food restaurant by local authorities in Prescott Valley, Arizona, on March 14, 2019, approximately four miles from this very street on Mallard Drive. It turns out my prediction was correct, and thankfully, he had not passed away as his mother had believed. Our prayers for his safe return have been answered.

Photo: This amazing sunset appeared after saying a full rosary in thanks for the safe return of Rilee Dennis to his family on March 16, 2019, near Sacred Heart Catholic Church in Prescott, Arizona, near Thumb Butte.

Photo: An amazing sunset from our Mother St. Mary over the skies of Prescott, Arizona, on March 27, 2019, after saying a rosary that morning asking for more signs from the skies and for our mother to bless our New Wine.

Photo: An amazing shot of the new sun with golden rays shining down on March 30, 2019, the day of my wife Carol's fiftieth birthday while hiking in Sedona, Arizona. Notice again another green orb present in the middle of the frame.

Photo: Another amazing shot of the new sun shining down with bending light rays on March 30, 2019, while hiking near Sedona, Arizona, for my wife Carol's fiftieth birthday. What the sun is doing here is something I've never seen in light and is beautiful beyond words. The first thing that comes to mind when I see this image is this: Lucifer equals "light bearer" and "light bender." This curvature of the sun's rays tells me his footprint is definitely present in Sedona, Arizona, a place of great beauty but also deep spiritual warfare.

Photo: Another amazing angel wing-like formation in the skies the morning of April 1, 2019, after saying an entire rosary at Sacred Heart Catholic Church in Prescott, Arizona, for world peace and for the world to embrace our two keys of "Be Love" and "Believe."

Photo: This amazing sunrise appeared the morning of April 4, 2019, the morning after my final press release for The New Wine Volume II: Peace Town was accepted and approved.

MESSAGES FROM MOTHER ST. MARY

Photo: An amazing sunset on the evening of April 9, 2019, the exact date the press release for The New Wine Volume II: Peace Town was sent out to thousands of media outlets worldwide. More confirmation from on high that this is the message given to us from our Mother St. Mary.

On November 2, 2018, a meteor exploded into a fireball over Arkansas.

On December 18, 2018, another school bus-sized meteor exploded over the Bering Sea with the force of 10 atomic bombs. That meteor weighed 1,500 tons and was 32 feet in diameter and traveling at 71,582 mph as it exploded over the ocean with a force of 173 kilotons of TNT.

On Monday, February 25, 2019, USA Today wrote an article entitled "Bomb Cyclone Strikes, Leaving over 650,000 without Power."

The bomb cyclone left 80 million civilians in over 14 states under a very high wind advisory with wind gusts up to 81 mph, which is hurricane force.

A "second bomb cyclone" then hit again in early March 2019. Heavy snowfall in Arizona (my new home state) left Flagstaff with over 35 inches of snow in one day, which is the single daily record for that city. Deadly tornadoes hit Mississippi and record flooding hit Tennessee.

The same day, yet another massive 7.5 earthquake struck Peru and more volcanic activity was recorded in Japan on February 25, 2019. Major volcanoes have erupted in Indonesia, Hawaii, and Mexico in 2018.

A few weeks prior to all of this saw west Michigan, my former home, witness a jaw dropping-67 degree below zero. As of February 27, 2019, two northern California towns have now been inundated with massive flooding, which has put them both underwater.

Between February 13 and February 25, 2019, a record 140 earthquakes hit the state of Utah, a predominantly Mormon state.

On March 3, 2019, fourteen people were killed by destructive tornadoes in Alabama that also hit Georgia.

On March 4, 2019, over a thousand commercial airline flights were canceled due to major ice and snow storms in the Northeast. St. Patrick's Day 2019 saw severe flooding in Nebraska, Missouri, and Kansas as the Missouri River Basin saw flooding in multiple states.

On March 18, 2019, the volcano in Mexico known as Popocatepetl exploded again in one of the largest eruptions seen in years. As of March 19, 2019, four very rare earthquakes have struck near the Florida-Alabama state line. As of March 21, 2019, another severe nor'easter is barreling in on the northeast coast of the United States.

On March 22, 2019, NOAA officially warned that severe flooding in 25 states may put the lives of over 200 million Americans at risk. On March 23, 2019 headlines revealed over 419 dead in Mozambique after a devastatingly powerful cyclone hit southern Africa.

On April 2, 2019 a third bomb cyclone was predicted to strike the northeast coast of the United States.

On April 15, 2019, the morning headlines read, "Notre Dame Cathedral Spire in Paris Collapses During Massive Fire."

On May 3, 2019, a record-setting cyclone hit the southeastern coast of India, placing the lives of over a million Indian citizens at risk.

On May 26, 2019, headlines read, "A hypersonic fireball just hit off the coast of Australia with the power of a nuclear weapon." This article detailed a meteor strike from May 21, 2019, as it passed the Coast of Australia.

The meteor entered the earth's atmosphere at over 25,000 mph and released enough energy equal to a small nuclear bomb. Also on May 26, 2019, a powerful magnitude 8.0 earthquake struck Peru.

On May 31, 2019, Mt. Etna erupted as a river of lava poured down the side of the mountain. On June 12, 2019, nearly 300,000 people were evacuated in India as another very powerful Cyclone Vanu approached the coastline.

On June 22, 2019, a volcano on the Russian island of Kuril exploded with such ferocity, it was videotaped by NASA from space. The eruption has contributed to a very unique occurrence of purple sunsets worldwide due to the release of sulfur. (Remember, purple is the color of royalty.) The volcano was last active in 1924. Also on June 22, 2019,

Australian headlines read, "Meteor lights up Queensland sky, leaving observers scared and amazed." Also on June 22, 2019, a second car-sized asteroid broke up 240 miles south of San Juan, Puerto Rico, as it exploded in a fireball releasing nearly 6,000 tons of TNT.

On June 29, 2019, at around 5:00 p.m., I observed a white, cylindrical object flying at what appeared to be over 35,000 feet in the sky. The object created no noise, had no discernible tail or wings, and left no contrail in the sky. As I took out my phone to try to capture it on video, the object completely disappeared without accelerating at all.

On July 3, 2019, a volcano erupted with an enormous ejection of fire and ash on the Italian island of Stromboli, killing at least one hiker. A day later, on July 4, 2019, as our nation celebrated its Independence Day, a strong 6.4 magnitude earthquake struck north Los Angeles, California. A day later, on July 5, 2019, an even stronger earthquake of magnitude 6.9 struck north Los Angeles, California, with greater force.

On July 13, 2019, Hurricane Barry slammed into the coast of Louisiana, eventually leaving tens of thousands without power.

On July 16, 2019, headlines in South Central Texas read, "Mysterious 'explosion' may be meteor," and detailed numerous reports of a loud bang in the early afternoon that rattled buildings.

On July 26, 2019, powerful storms left over half a million people without power across Wisconsin and Michigan.

On August 11, 2019, another volcano erupted near Tokyo, Japan, forcing evacuations.

On August 12, 2019, headlines read, "Tornadoes set to strike Britain as locals warned of freak storms." Days later, headlines read that the month of July 2019 was the hottest month on record in earth's history. As of mid-August 2019, fires have ravaged most of the Amazon rainforest and its life-giving plants and rare organisms. While the Amazon rainforest was the greatest protection we had against carbon dioxide buildup, it is now contributing to higher levels of carbon dioxide release from these fires.

On August 28, 2019, the Stromboli volcano erupted anew in Italy as Hurricane Dorian started lowering in pressure on its way toward the Florida coastline. On the morning of August 29, 2019, a 6.3 magnitude earthquake struck off the coast of Oregon.

Also on August 29, 2019, headlines read, "Month of storm hell with torrential rain and gales to smash Britain."

On August 30, 2019, a new ominous "black moon" will appear in our skies.

On September 20, 2019, headlines reported that six tropical storms had formed in the Atlantic and Pacific Oceans, tying a record from September 1992. Also, on September 20, 2019, headlines reported that the Sakurajima volcano in Japan had erupted, sending ash miles into the sky.

On September 24, 2019, tropical storm Karen made its way toward Puerto Rico, the same day a 6.0 magnitude earthquake struck the island commonwealth.

On September 26, 2019, a 6.8 magnitude earthquake struck Indonesia, killing at least 30 people.

On September 27, 2019, NASA reported that an asteroid about the size of a double-decker London bus hurtled dangerously close to the earth at over 9,200 mph.

On September 29, 2019, headlines reported that a second category 5 hurricane named Lorenzo had set a record for the strongest hurricane in the Eastern Atlantic in history.

On September 29, 2019, a strong 6.8 magnitude earthquake struck the coast of Chile.

On October 2, 2019, the Poas Volcano erupted in Costa Rica, forcing evacuations.

On October 7, 2019, Typhoon Hagibis turned from a tropical storm to category 5 monster in eighteen hours, setting a record. Also on October 7, 2019, NASA reported monitoring sixteen asteroids moving at tremendous speeds with trajectories bringing them close to earth. Many scientists have theorized that the magnetic pole shift has already happened due to Nibiru's pass and has contributed to some of these apocalyptic events and that many of these meteors and asteroids are from the tail of the red dwarf second sun referred to as "the red dragon" in the prophecy from 95 AD (the woman clothed in the sun).

Photo: Hurricane Dorian, as it heads toward the US East Coast on Labor Day Weekend 2019. Dorian, a category 5 hurricane, has the distinction of being the strongest- recorded hurricane in modern history with winds pushing 200 mph. One meteorologist stated he had never seen a hurricane behave like Dorian where it would stop and not move in any direction.

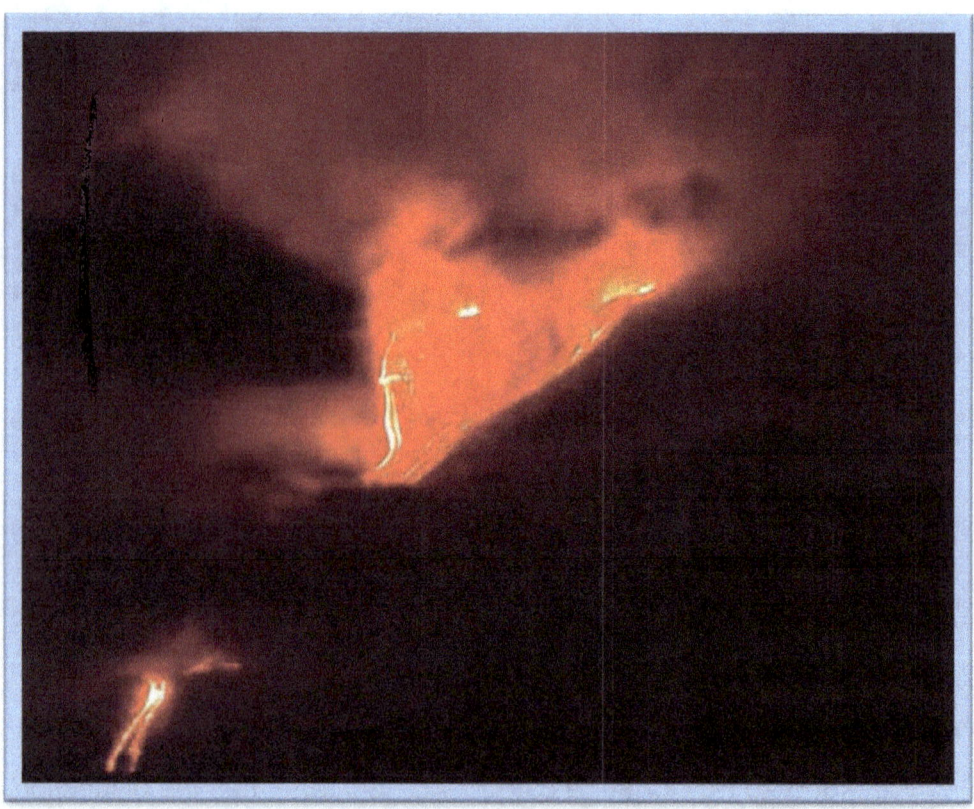

Photo: An amazing image of Mt. Etna erupting on May 31, 2019, as a river of lava pours down the side of the mountain.

Photo: An amazing photo of a bolt of lightning striking inside an erupting volcano in Russia in mid-August 2019, signaling a new beginning or apocalypse.

Photo: An amazing photo taken by my wife Carol in the skies above Prescott Valley, Arizona, on August 14, 2019, the night of the "sturgeon moon." The name sturgeon moon originated with the Native Americans of the Great Lakes area in the Midwest, and it means a spiritual rebirth or new beginning, especially for those who have endured long suffering. Another reference again to an apocalypse or new beginning.

A few days after our new sturgeon moon appeared, I was running in our neighborhood near Prescott Valley, Arizona, and ran by my neighbor who was walking his golden retriever. I said to him, "Her name is Sadie, right?" He looked at me flabbergasted and said, "No, her name is Emmy, but my last dog that died was named Sadie."

You should have seen the look on his face. I had to explain my gift of clairvoyance to him. This is the type of spiritual rebirth that a sturgeon moon brings even for golden retrievers named Sadie.

Does anyone dispute that we are definitively in the Book of Revelations or the apocalypse? Why is no one asking him why these things are happening and how do we stop them as one people in one world from continuing? Is this because no one wants change in this world? No one wants a planet where everyone is equally fed and clothed and sheltered? Does anyone want to continue to live under the constant threat of nuclear annihilation?

Boynton Canyon

Photo: This is a very intriguing image taken in February 2019. This was taken while on a hike near Boynton Canyon in Sedona, Arizona, near the Enchantment Resort. Conspiracy theorist David Icke lists this resort as a possible "alien reptilian underground base." At first, I thought this notion to be absurd, considering it would be very difficult to hide such a large operation underground without locals uncovering it. However, these very strange painted crosses which seem to mock or at the very least reference the crucifixion of Jesus Christ on Calvary seem very out of place for the area and extremely odd. Could these be used to hold off angelic forces by "alien reptilians" and other fallen angels/demons who follow the other lion of the night Lucifer/Hillel Ben Shachar/Memnoch/Satan/red dragon/devil? There is without a doubt major spiritual warfare being waged near Sedona, Arizona.

To reinforce the notion of major spiritual warfare being waged in Arizona, I will relay a brief story about a former FBI agent we met on our first night staying in Prescott, Arizona. The first morning at our motel, our chocolate Lab—German shorthaired pointer mix, Reese, accidentally locked himself in our U-Haul. The gentleman who arrived to assist us in unlocking the vehicle was a former FBI agent named John McVeigh. John divulged he was actually the cousin of Timothy McVeigh, the infamous Oklahoma City Bomber. After chatting briefly with John about our shared military backgrounds, he informed us that his uncle was still in the FBI and had dozens of videos to include surveillance videos at convenience stores of citizens being abducted by a fast-moving white light.

Such disappearances would be described as alien abduction, but they also bear some similarities to descriptions of the biblical rapture as well when Jesus stated that at his return there will be two women in a field and that "one will be taken and one will be left." We certainly seem to be living in apocalyptic times that have fulfilled prophecies from centuries ago regarding the return of the Christian kingdom.

Photo: This amazing sunset near Prescott Valley, Arizona, was waiting for us on the evening of April 14, 2019, after hiking all day near Devil's Bridge in Sedona, Arizona. This was taken the day of Palm Sunday 2019 and is further proof to me of both the other kingdom being a "sun dome in the night" and protection from the angels and saints on high.

Photo: This amazing sunset photo was taken the evening of April 18, 2019, near Prescott Valley, Arizona. I looked up online the spiritual significance of the day of April 18th, and curiously enough, April 18, 1506, marked the dedication of the cornerstone at St. Peter's Basilica Catholic Church at the Vatican in Rome. This event occurred 513 years ago, which is a spiritually significant angelic number, signifying reward of abundance following struggle.

Photo: An amazing image taken at an Easter brunch in Sedona, Arizona, on April 21, 2019, following an Easter Mass at St. John Vianney Catholic Church in Sedona, Arizona. I took this image to represent the three sons of St. Mary that have incarnated in the last two thousand years represented in a cloud formation.

Photo: This incredible sunset photo was taken the evening of April 30, 2019, near Prescott Valley, Arizona, after a day of numerous rosary prayers for world peace and for this world to embrace our two keys of "Be Love" and "Believe." This view of the "other kingdom" is simply spectacular.

Photo: This incredible sunset appeared in the skies above Prescott Valley, Arizona, on May 2, 2019, the evening before a record-setting cyclone hit the eastern coast of India.

Photo: An incredible faint rainbow breaks across the skies near Prescott Valley, Arizona, on May 27, 2019, Memorial Day. This rainbow appears to hit the top of a steeple on another nearby church. This appeared after a morning rosary focusing on world peace and for the world to turn away from greed and war.

Photo: The evening of September 7, 2019, a pair of fraternal twin rainbows near the skies of Prescott Valley, Arizona.

Photo: My amazing coworker Kristina who helps to stomp out blindness daily at our job of selling products for retinal surgeries. She told me an incredible story of her own birth in which a mysterious woman appeared out of nowhere to inform her mother that this "child must be named Kristina," after doctors gave her mother little hope of her surviving. The hospital had no record of this mystery woman working there. Kristina was born in Russia, a communist country, on a date that celebrates Jesus Christ. The people believe that all water is holy on this day, including water in the womb.

Photo: This amazing photograph of the setting sun over Phoenix, Arizona, on June 5, 2019, the same evening my coworker Kristina said to me, "Hey, we never got our sunset from Mary." This was after I had promised a beautiful dancing sunset for us both from our mother St. Mary the same day. Looks like St. Mary delivered for us all.

Photo: Another beautiful sunrise near Phoenix, Arizona, on the morning my new coworker Kristina who has an amazing birth story related to the other kingdom was set to return to the valley of the sun to help stomp out blindness.

Photo: An amazing dancing sunset the night of June 23, 2019, near our home of Prescott Valley, Arizona.

Photo: An amazing sunset the night of June 23, 2019, near our home of Prescott Valley, Arizona. The sun was dancing before it fell from sight leaving this amazing multicolored bands of rich hues.

Photo: Another amazing sunset near Prescott Valley, Arizona, on June 25, 2019.

Photo: Another mysterious and beautiful sunset near Prescott, Arizona, the night of June 29, 2019, after having dinner with my wife Carol Rose and also after witnessing a UFO high above the skies near Prescott Valley, Arizona, earlier in the evening.

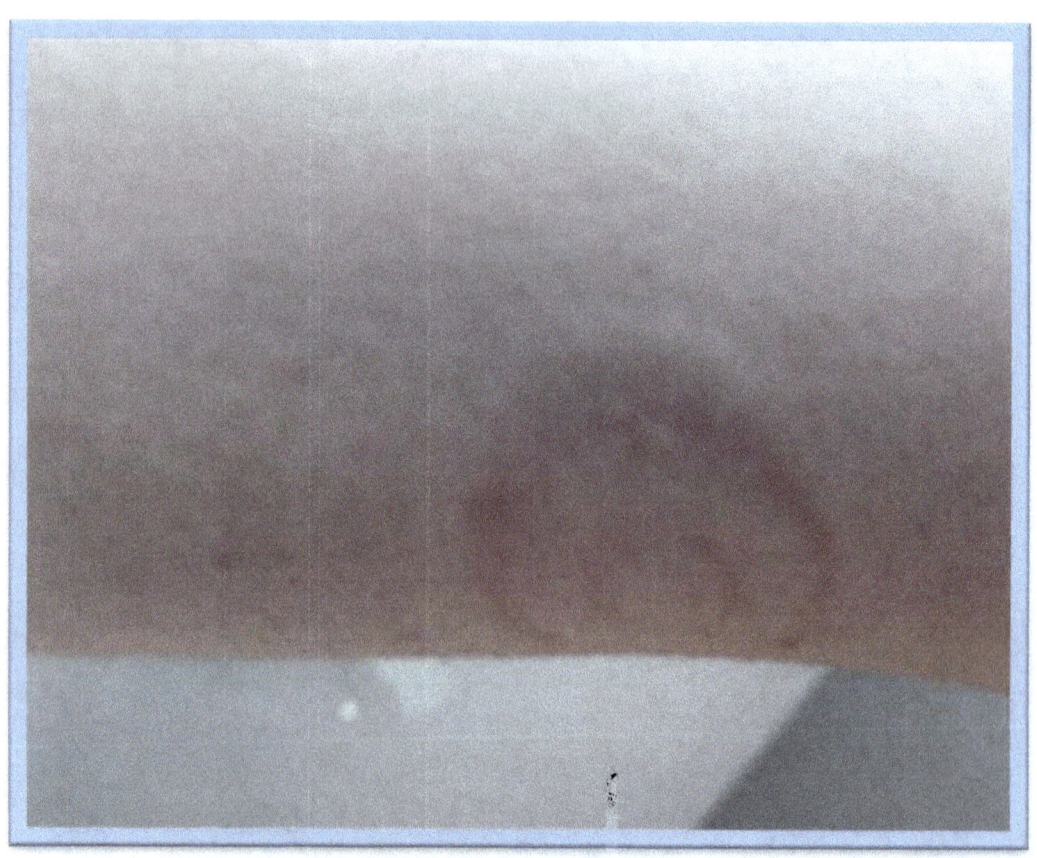

Photo: A very unusual red mark on the underside of my wife Carol's arm right before seeing my first ever UFO in the skies above our home in June 2019. You can clearly see a circle surrounded by another circle. The image was raised and red and literally appeared out of nowhere. We have no explanation for its appearance, but it disappeared soon after. We could find no objects in our home that could have made such a mark.

Photo: Another amazing sunset the evening of July 3, 2019, on our way to Page, Arizona, for an Independence Day minivacation.

Photo: Another amazing sunset near Prescott Valley, Arizona, on June 25, 2019.

Photo: Another mysterious and beautiful sunset near Prescott, Arizona, the night of June 29, 2019, after having dinner with my wife Carol Rose and also after witnessing a UFO high above the skies near Prescott Valley, Arizona, earlier in the evening.

Photo: Our Navajo Nation tour guide Justin, who is a full-breed Navajo Native American, on July 4, 2019. We bonded immediately due to my shared Cherokee heritage. I called him my brother from another tribe. Justin offered amazing insight into the spiritual realm. He stated to me he has personally witnessed UFOs on his reservation that his elders describe as spirits or green orb lights that move early at dawn at high rates of speed. His tribe believes these are spirits of tribal members who have passed on to the other side.

Photo: Justin gave us a tour of Antelope Canyon near Page, Arizona, on July 4, 2019. This rock formation, which was carved by natural elements of wind, water, and heat, shows what his tribe describes as the face of an Indian chief. If you look closely enough, you will see a face with a wide-open mouth in traditional headdress.

Photo: Another amazing shot from deep in Antelope Canyon near Page, Arizona, on native Navajo tribal land on July 4, 2019. This image shows what our guide Justin described to us as a bald eagle head in flight in the middle of the frame.

Photo: Another amazing shot from deep inside Antelope Canyon near Page, Arizona, on the Navajo reservation on July 4, 2019. This shot is described by our tour guide Justin as a lion's face seen in the bottom middle of the frame.

Photo: The "left jaw" of St. Mary, James Douglas Morrison, circa 1962 as a high school senior, future leader of The Doors musical group.

Photo: The "right jaw" of St. Mary, Matthew Douglas Pinard, circa 1992 while a senior in high school and author of The New Wine series of books. I believe myself to be the reincarnation of James Douglas Morrison and his fraternal twin and half-brother who, when we are both spiritually conjoined via St. Mary, represent Dionysus, the god of wine and fertility, also incarnate and immortal. Jesus Christ was also Dionysus incarnate. Jim is always with me, and we are never apart throughout time. We are conjoined, fraternal twins. We come from the other kingdom of heaven and are referred to as "lurking jaws, joints in time."

Photo: In the evening hours of July 16, 2019, this extremely odd light appeared in the skies above our home near Prescott Valley, Arizona. My wife Carol took a nearly forty second video of this light darting across the skies changing both its size and shape and also changing its intensity of illumination. The object also accelerated at rates of speed that are beyond any technology on earth. The object also shrank to a very small bright white light before exploding like fireworks and disappearing from view only to reappear shortly after. It is one of the most amazing videos I have ever seen, and I definitely trust the source. I forwarded the video to a local news station. I was traveling for work on this day and did not witness it in person, but it is unlike any phenomenon I have ever witnessed before.

Photo: On July 19, 2019, the exact date of the eleventh wedding anniversary of St. Mary's New Rose (my wife Carol) and her New Wine (myself), this beautiful sunset appeared over the skies of Prescott Valley, Arizona.

Photo: In recent recitations of the full rosary, I say every day for world peace, I had also asked our Mother Mary to bring Paxton back to this world. This very peculiar photo appeared above the skies of our new home near Prescott Valley, Arizona, on the evening of August 4, 2019. My wife's immediate comment was that it looked like a baby or fetus inside a womb like you would see on an ultrasound near the bottom right half of the frame. I'm not sure if Paxton will rejoin us or not, but anything is possible with God the Father.

Photo: Another beautiful sunset above Prescott Valley, Arizona, on August 5, 2019, after prayers to Mother Mary for world peace and for the world to accept our New Wine.

Photo: On August 16, 2019, I was fortunate enough to see a public screening of The Doors: The Final Cut and meet an old friend, Doors drummer John Densmore, who graciously signed his book for me. It was thoroughly amusing to me listening to John and Oliver Stone joke earlier in the evening from the stage about Jim being definitely still alive and probably in the audience this evening.

Photo: An amazing sunset the evening of August 28, 2019, over the skies of Prescott Valley, Arizona. To me, this cloud appears like the face of an animal, perhaps a dog, with the sun's rays shooting out from the eye socket. A cross seems to be hanging down from its neck near the bottom of the cloud. It is breathtakingly beautiful. As I've always joked to family and friends, dog = God.

Photo: Another image of the sunset-lit clouds above Prescott Valley, Arizona, on August 28, 2019, that's also breathtakingly beautiful. I would call this image "God's Pillow," perhaps where he rests his head.

Photo: Another amazing sunset the evening of August 29, 2019, in the skies above Prescott Valley, Arizona.

Photo: Another amazing sunset the evening of September 3, 2019, after saying a rosary that morning for the safety of friends and family in Florida. I asked St. Mary to use the Father's breath to "push hurricane Dorian back out to sea."

Photo: A meteor streaks across the night sky in September 2019, illuminating the countless stars above.

Photo: The evening of September 14, 2019, brought a very apocalyptic type of monsoon storm above the skies of Prescott Valley, Arizona, with rain showers and lightning strikes.

Photo: The morning of September 15, 2019, brought us a unique visitor to our front door. A yellow butterfly signifies resurrection, prosperity, hope, and change in the Christian faith. It also signals exciting things are on the horizon. I pray this butterfly is here for the entire world.

Photo: During midafternoon in the skies above Prescott Valley, Arizona, on September 15th, after a day at Sacred Heart Catholic Church celebrating mass and saying a full rosary for world peace—this remarkable cloud formation appeared with what looks like a very large angel wing on top.

Photo: An abnormal sunset the evening before another "bomb cyclone" was predicted to hit the west coast of the United States. I clearly see a demonic looking face in the clouds with a goatee and nose and dark circles as eyes. I have shown this image to family members and friends and we all concur this is the face once again of Lucifer/ Hillel Ben Shachar/Memnoch/Satan/Red Dragon/Devil. I am hoping this is a sign he is safely far from all of us. This appeared on the evening of November 26, 2019 as I had just received word The New Wine Volume III was being finalized for publication.

Photo: On the evening of Wednesday, November 27th, 2019 this incredibly beautiful sunset appeared in the skies above Prescott Valley, Arizona on the night before Thanksgiving Day. I found it fascinating that I see no demonic faces in this sunset and pray this is a turning point for the entire world.

Photo: This amazing sunrise was photographed on my way to Rosary Prayers at St. Germaine Catholic Church in Prescott Valley, Arizona on the morning of Friday,

December 6th, 2019. December 6th is a very important date in the Catholic Church as it celebrates St. Nicholas Day. St. Nicholas is the patron Saint of Russia and Greece and is noted for his generosity. I am taking this sunrise as a sign of great things to come for this world.

TAXI ARCH

Photo: This amazing sunrise occurred the morning of December 18, 2019 exactly one year to the day after a meteor exploded 16 miles above the Bering Sea unleashing 173 Kilotons of energy which is ten times the power of the atomic bomb dropped on Hiroshima, Japan in World War II.

I continue to pray to all the angels and saints in the other kingdom and to our Mother Mary for world peace and for this world to disarm all weapons of mass destruction and turn away from greed. I also pray for God's protection of all of us from the demonic "lions of the night" in the service of the dark one Lucifer/Hillel Ben Shachar/ Memnoch/Satan/Red Dragon/Devil. I would like to end this third volume of The New Wine with an original prayer I use daily and a new original poem entitled "Taxi Arch" in honor of St. Michael the Arch Angel as he continues to battle the "lions of the night" as well as a famous quote from my half-brother James. I will let my readers figure out the meaning of both.

"When the True King's Murderers are allowed to roam free a thousand magicians rise up in the land..." —James Douglas Morrison

Taxi Arch

An original poem by
Matthew Douglas Pinard and James Douglas Morrison
Dedicated to the memory of Saint Michael "Mystify Me" Hutchence

Brigadier you are, Saint Michael, Taxi Arch, ruler of worlds, seer of all On
Sunday you came down, a wing walker across your cloud standing tall

Defender in battle raging with light as the
arrow strung firmly across your bow
Slinging truth, love, and a sun
striking fast into the heart of the dark one now
A triple stacked Son spreading
his two keys, one love, the other believe
Scattered shepherds Sons,
Veil Rent in the land free, fire flows like a sieve
A choir now sings, of two Kingdoms
still being, both dimensions bereave
Souls now flying straight to their King who
holds three rings as Mary sings
Saint Barbara, the Old Mission, a painted
prophecy come true in cloak of blue
Floating on clouds, crimson red, the
Sons not dead, but rather they are three
Next to many half-breeds, angels with their wings,
witnessing the Mother Queen
Disciples, Apostles, carrying a cross held high with wings,
Adonai has been

The all seeing Eye of Horus reclaimed for the
Kingdom of Light remade
Sunsets, sunrises never before seen,
souls departing lay claim to the wing
Of Taxi Arch Michael and Saint Gabriel,
Peace Town, our Mother not grieved
For now they see, a colored iris not deceived,
windows into souls seeking to be
A new wine, old skins into new ones,
vibrations heightened to levels foreseen
Angels and Saints precede a Super Sturgeon
Moon being the light of three
Fault lines do shake, opening like torn leaves,
showing where faults lie
Volcanic ash into the sky as the Taxi Arch
brings His Apocalypse on high

I've heard some local Christian radio broadcasts stating there is presently a desire to learn how to pray among many believers. I am going to also enclose the main prayer that I say every single day, sometimes twice a day, before my full rosary. I always say this prayer directed to St. Mary as she is the Woman of the Apocalypse and it goes like this:

Ashen Lady (St. Mary) give up your vows,
save our city, right now: Ashanti Anunnaki Adonai
Ashanti Anunnaki Angel (pronounce this "An" "Hell")
Ashanti Anunnaki Sancti
In Shalla mama Mary, hear the voice of your son (or daughter)

I ask you to ask my Father to grant unto this world our two keys
Bring peace to this world, bring this world to disarm and turn from greed
Show us signs from the skies, wrap us all in your Arch's wings

May this world embrace your Son,
may this world come to Our Father
May this world turn away from the
Dark One and may our Kingdom Come
Abandon not your son (or daughter),
bind all the lions of the night
With our New Wine
May our new sun shine
down from our Sundome

Of light in the middle of dark night, bring this prayer on eagle's wings
Find my Father's house and his ear, and may Elijah's healing rays
Find their mark and change dark hearts in order to grant us wings
May this world embrace Be Love and Believe and trust in your thief

About the Author

Matthew Douglas Pinard is the author of The New Wine series. He was born and raised in southeastern Michigan and has a bachelor's degree in psychology from the University of Michigan and a master's degree in military history from Louisiana State University. Matthew is also a former US Army JAG legal specialist. He and his wife Carol Rose are recent transplants from west Michigan and now live in beautiful Prescott Valley, Arizona, with their two dogs Reese, a chocolate Lab, and Cleetus, a Redbone Coonhound. Matthew is a ranked Shihan (sixth degree) in Hakko Den shin Ryu Japanese Jujutsu and enjoys hiking, communing with the other side, praying for world peace, and photographing archangels in his spare time. Matthew Douglas Pinard and James Douglas Morrison (734) 649-8431 / pinardm@gmail.com

Other Books by Author Matthew

matthewpinardauthor.com

Follow Me:

- Goodreads
- Author Central
- YouTube

Screenplay Awards Matthew Douglas Pinard

Official Selection

Bloodstained Indie Film Festival

StoryPros Awards Screenplay Contest

Military Script Showcase

L.A. Neo Noir Novel Film & Script Festival

True Story International Film Festival

Reel Heart International Film Festival

Hollywood Boulevard International Film Festival

Independent Talents International Film Festival

Fort Worth Indie Film Showcase

California Independent Film Festival

San Pedro International Film Festival,

Southeastern International Film Festival

Louisiana International Film Festival

Official Selection

First Ten Pages Script Contest

Atlanta Comedy Film Festival

Georgia Shorts Film Festival

Official Finalist

Las Vegas International Film and Screenwriting Contest,
Honorable Mention

Depth of Field International Film Festival, Award Winner

Beverly Hills International Film Festival, Silver Winner

Queen Palm International Film Festival, Award Winner

Colorado International Film Festival, Quarter-Finalist

Chicago Screenplay Awards, Quarter-Finalist

NYC International Screenplay Awards, Quarter-Finalist

Atlanta Screenplay Awards, Semi-Finalist

Cordillera International Film Festival, Semi-Finalist

Fade In Awards, Finalist

Breaking Walls Thriller Screenplay Award Winner

Vegas Movie Awards,

The Santa Barbara International Screenplay Awards, Finalist

Miami Screen Play Awards, Quarter-Finalist:

www.ingramcontent.com/pod-product-compliance
Lightning Source LLC
Chambersburg PA
CBHW081357070526
44583CB00020B/2585